# Poems for Old Guys

Bill Kelly

Photography
Jennifer Thompson

Book Design
Susan Sezgin

*For Lynn & Rick,
In respect and admiration
for your special ways of loving
and courage in living.
Bill
8/16/17*

Also by Bill Kelly:
**Kindness is In Me,** Poems in Praise of Men (2012)

Copyright © 2017 by Bill Kelly

All rights reserved. No part of this book may be reproduced in any manner without the express written consent of the author, except in the case of brief excerpts in critical reviews and articles. For information, contact Bill Kelly at billkelly815@gmail.com.

Excerpt from "East Coker" from FOUR QUARTETS by T.S. Eliot. Copyright 1940 by T.S. Eliot. Copyright© renewed 1968 by Esme Valerie Eliot. Reprinted by permission of Houghton Mifflin Harcourt Publishing Company. All rights reserved.

## Table of Contents

### Why "Poems for Old Guys"?

| | |
|---|---|
| Fragility | 1 |
| In-between Time | 3 |
| Alternative Creation Story | 5 |
| Being Prayer | 7 |
| 47 The View From Here | 9 |
| On The Road | 11 |
| Catch Up | 13 |
| Infinity | 15 |
| No Words Come | 17 |
| Retirement Party - His | 19 |
| "Take it Easy" | 21 |
| Coming Near My 59th Birthday | 23 |
| "She Looks Like My Wife" | 25 |
| How to Delay Going Crazy | 27 |
| My Pictures of Gallucci | 29 |
| My 69th Birthday Poem | 31 |
| Coming To The End | 33 |
| Beloved, Help Me Find the Words | 35 |
| Time (or At My 50th High School Reunion) | 37 |
| Reality Check | 39 |
| Sun River Plunge | 41 |
| Grief | 43 |
| What Do I Feel For You? | 45 |
| Prayer? | 47 |
| Beauties | 49 |
| Thank You Friends | 51 |
| Vulnerability | 53 |
| Spring Train to Portland | 55 |
| Holy Water | 57 |
| Who You Are In Me | 59 |
| Our Forest Cabin | 60 |
| Joan - Celebrating Her Life | 63 |

## Dedication

Giving thanks for the fierce and loving guidance
of "old guys" I have known
Howard, Herb, Larkin, Bix, Mel, Mike, and
Bob, my dad.

Old men ought to be explorers
Here and there does not matter
We must be still and still moving
Into another intensity
For another union, deeper communion

T.S. Eliot, "East Coker"

## Why "Poems for Old Guys"?

Aging is like writing a poem:
slow enough to feel the rhythm
expect repetition -
see revision of time.

My life unfolded of its own:
a path traveled in steps.
Perspective revealing its
mysterious interior terrain.

I learned: words are for feelings
facts can't contain.
Energy - like time - for savoring
won't come again.

Few choices remain:
do I leave a legacy in money or stone?
Plow on to the end, bitter, alone?
Waste away in grief for all undone?

What, writ within
now draws these tears?
Opening my heart,
trusting this invitation to...

## Fragility

Walking in a September forest
I caught leaves as they came
Falling like a golden rain

One leaf floated to rest
On a lower limb
A little gift to me

Light as life
Beauty in my palm
Dry, whole, calm

Lived this season
Feeding its tree
Now teaching me

### In-between Time

The bright sun
seems further away.
But creek flows.
Grass grows.

Winds blow, leaves dance
gold against a blue blue sky.
Clouds drift like sailboats
taking silent soundings.

The breeze
carries a new edge
leaving only memory
of warmth gone by.

Leaves sound drier –
an old woman's hands.
Clouds now dark battleships
gathering for combat.

I have entered the
has been
not yet
time.

In-between:
questioning   answering
growing       knowing
leaving       arriving.

Awaiting.

## Alternative Creation Story

Out of time
God made the human mind
human
from materials at hand.

When she got to the heart
God saw there was not enough
of the stuff
to complete this part.

It was inspiration -
not collaboration -
that only a piece of
herself would do.

Which is why -
to this day -
we cannot comprehend our end
only feel our way.

## Being Prayer

The rooftop is what
God
sees first.
Then my bald head.
Uninvited He comes
like the man lowered through the roof,
wholly inhabiting me.

OR

She flies in with an F147 roar
that shuts out everything
filling up my mind.
Taking me over
by emptying me out.

OR

I think:
"Maybe I do this one more chore,
then I'll pray."
It never works –
there is always another angel to wrestle.

OR

The silence pushes out voices and tasks.
A painful silence
- so loud it hurts -
shrinks the distance between us.
Embracing me in stillness.

AND

At special times, like now,
The Holy comes up like a tide.
I just sit at my chair -
full of Enough, empty of stuff -
and float.

# 47
## The View From Here

I see the death of my ideals
And the reality of my finiteness

I recognize pain in others' lives
My experience softens judgment

I feel small, the world seems big again
I discover God outside of church

My toenails are cracking, hair is going
I learn about dying

I see my career track in new perspective
I'm sliding off it

I walk the beach creating,
At last,
my own path on this strand.

## On The Road

Gas stations
were Service Stations
now they are Mini-marts
but EasyStops
don't change tires or
answer questions of direction.

Have I gone the way of gas stations:
        lost my usefulness?
        given up on service?
        opted for easy anonymity?

On this trip I get confused about what I'm for:
        I know what I do –
        but what am I here to do?
        how do I fit with others?

Many say that meaning comes from doing
others say doing comes from meaning
few say there is no meaning
no matter.

Today I see no service stations.
I'm traveling with uneasy urgency –
like a filling bladder –
of questions.

## Catch Up

Pumping pedals furiously
I look back over my shoulder
Seeing what I fear.

Not death – worse –
Not being me
I push on, out of my skin.

Stretched like a bad actor
I look to others for my cue
Stand awkwardly at my spot.

How old will I be
When who I was
Catches up with who I need to be?

My past
Will catch me
In my future.

## Infinity

If I write this line
there will be an end to it.
Or

I could publish a blank sheet
but the page would have edges
and strange reviews.

Better I describe the meteor shower :
    South Brother Peak
    deep among Olympic Mountains,
    no lights, no moon, only
    stars and silver sparks shooting
    into black velvet depths.

Just like in the closet long ago
with my dear brother
and toy guns that sparkle.

I am inside the whole.
Included, possibly glimpsing
where he too soon did go.

## No Words Come

When in the course
of very human events

> - an autumnal walk
> in the evening forest
> with my partner in 42 married years,
> green mountain before us
> gold lit by a setting sun,
> as the full moon
> surprises -

I am moved, hushed, humbled, then impelled
to create, write, sing, declare something…..!
No words come.

I find no way, no how,
no row or column to contain this show
no words to name what stirs inside.

"Bigger than me, yet in me, in us… . "
A beginning
or a prayer?

## Retirement Party – His

First guests look old
I suddenly want to be in a cave
In India
Far from the damages of aging
And endings.

Truth of the evening bears on -
As it does -
Bathing the moment in sacred sunset colors
As nostalgic blue clouds float far north
Leaving me a clear preview of my own reality.

When I was a boy
I thought retirement
Was a kind of death.
His guests speak of new stages and
Adventures, trails to explore.

Some pause in hesitation, question:
*"Who's next?"*
In this evening's alpenglow a daunting refrain:
Yield the past
Future to gain.

## "Take It Easy!"

Alright:
I know the installer lies
when he says, "It's easy."

Even my friend says "No sweat,
this'll be easy,"
but I end up wheezy.

The doc, dentist, gardener,
each say "Take it easy," yet
when the bills come I get dizzy.

Even my lover whispers
in my ear
"Easy, easy…"

What I want to know is
**HOW**
to take it easy?

## Coming Near My 59th Birthday

This morning my wife said,
    "We should put in our will
    who gets your grandma's rocker
    and your dad's desk –

    who will hold for your family
    enough care
    to accept the embroidered pillowcase
    of the Irish dandy."
*Is it already time to let go?*
*Is it past time to accept I've never had an answer?*

This afternoon
In the office we sat with two young couples,
each with their own version of summer:
    "Three months from hell."
    "A time of endings and beginnings, both of love."

This evening
Still confused
I asked the gray squirrel that came for dinner.
She heard me.
I could feel in her black attentive eyes she heard me.

My questions disappeared
in the universe of her deep gaze.
I felt small.
Wisely, she kept her council.

# "She Looks Like My Wife"
## Eulogy for My Best Friend

Over the years John said to me
This one sentence
full of meaning
but never the same:

-In college when we saw Karen for the first time.

-Soon after the birth of their daughter.

-At the celebration of their granddaughter's graduation

-Seeing a woman in the crowd after Karen's death

-His generic greeting to visitors to his Alzheimer's unit

-A figure he said was waiting for him "on the other side"
when I saw him last.

I was a guest on a slow train
through John's loving life
that had no borders or boundaries
he widened the view for me.

## How to Delay Going Crazy

(With apologies to H.W. Longfellow and Wendell Berry)

When my memory stick gets stuck,
The RAM's gone missing,
And the back up is backed up backed up backed up....

OR

When I find myself on
The dead limb of a phone tree
With jumping off the only selection

THEN

I cold turkey withdraw from the CRT
Or ATT (as the case may be) and
Get me down to the sea.

I walk long on the sand
And find relief in the demand:
Next time 'round I should be an otter.

## My Pictures of Gallucci

Standing in the sun
Tall, smiling, waving
In front of King Center

Bending down to lift
Curly red haired girl
In his arms on G street

Stretching out in gray fog
Strong, firm, and scared
In front of white train

Calling, organizing, teaching
Hungering, thirsting, persisting
Seeking justice: here now

Jogging his neighborhood
Passing yellow home full of history and hurt
Trying to warm the silent distance within it
Seeking his soul's way out.

Confused old man dressed in hospital white
Bedded between sacred and science
Staring up into my hope
Renewing my passion for this life.

## My 69th Birthday Poem

We are old at different ages
a transforming process:
       reading glasses,
       hair line and
       memory receeding.

Young 'old people'
teach me to live with:
       death
       cancer
       roller coasters.

They became chrysalis:
       gained by dying
       learned by flying
       began again.

*Now*
catches my attention:
       sharpens focus
       reorders priorities
       widens horizon.

## Coming To The End

Coming to the end is a scary proposition:
No room to negotiate or reposition
No words delay my transition.
"Later" is now this last situation.

We live on either side of present:
Locked in summer photos,
Lost in Fall colors,
Or next Spring's garden.

We deny Winter's call,
Wake too late,
Quit too soon,
We have not lived at all.

Today I commit not knowing
I let down my defense,
Welcome fear, joy, and
Open to life's flowing.

# Beloved
# Help Me With Words

Help me find words:
for the aching in my soul,
loss of one not yet grieved,
my tender mix of pride and proud.

Help find a way
to open up my heart
to what lives between love and like
or discover jealousy's start.

Help me say
what prompts my tears
when surprised by warmth in a winter's day
or I lie within your arms.

Help me abandon words
when I am closer to truth or
reach for sacred mysteries
beyond my grasp.

# Time
## or
## At My 50th High School Reunion

What is this racing my heart?
Out of place – dropped back in time –
I find myself walking around
in my history.

I see my young face, framed by time
open, innocent, smiling
insecurely: ivy league shirts and after shave.

I turn around to find
wrinkles, bags, and sags.
Gravity's done its work, while
Life has done its time.

Behind bifocals, I feel 18
yet friends beside me
gently bring me back to now.

Here I catch reflections
of my disbelief, confusion, questions.
I am sparked by a mischief long remembered;
touched by words of worn wisdom.

I feel grasps of desperation, isolation,
thick insulation; see humility, creativity,
courage before pain, grief after loss.

Deep in the darkness of my pocket
holding our simple rings
I am filled by gratitude for this moment and
graced continuity of our time.

## Reality Check

Today I am at the DMV
waiting, like everyone else,
for my number to be called.
No: "premium service" for me,
    friend on the inside, or
    padded chair.

I need to renew my license
sitting, like everybody else,
next to people I'd never meet
who are speaking strange languages,
    wearing pajamas, and
    ignoring me.

I try to make use of my time
writing this poem
but, like everybody else
I watch the children:
    playing, drawing, running, talking
    not like anybody else.

When my number is called
the man doesn't thank me for
my clean record or organ donation.
He wants the $25 required of everybody else
    cash, check,
    Visa, or MasterCard.

The lady doesn't tell me
when to smile for the photo
so for the next ten years
I'll be:
    bored,
    like everybody else.

As I walk out to my car -
through the smokers at the door -
I feel a strangely freeing sensation:
    I'd slipped from who I was
    and been everybody else.

## Sun River Plunge

Sometimes
down, down, down –
tossed about by life's dare -
is up.

Today this old man dove into the cold river
and up came
the happy kid
who had been double dared

*-and here is the important part –*

by his older,
neverdoanythingwrong, brother
to jump into Snow Lake
during a November Scouting trip.

And the kid – *righthenandthere* - did!
Up he came
with a brand new kind of "happy"
in himself

that he wanted more of
and he did
and I did again
today!

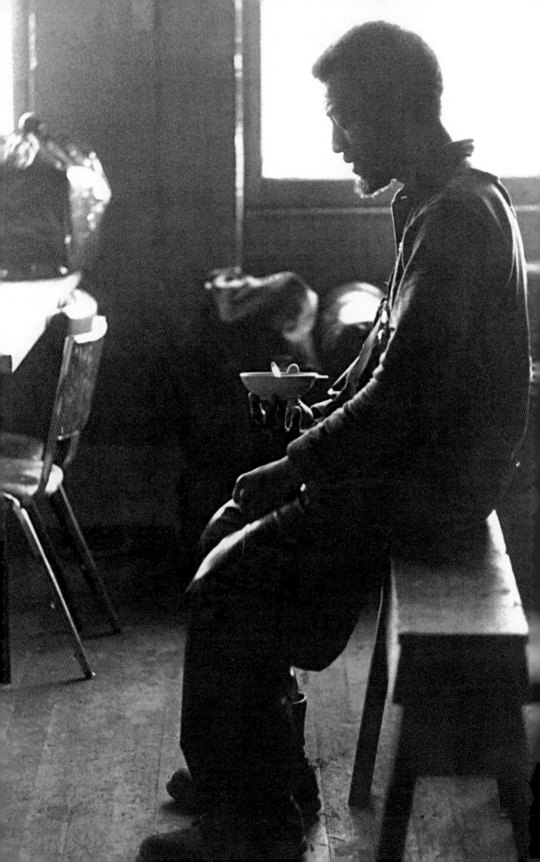

# Grief

How do I love
When I cannot help?
When "being involved"
Complicates the complexity
Of my lover's living?

How do I listen
When there is no end
To your condition –
No solution sticks?

Where do I put my grief
As I watch you wither
Away years, lose
Your spark under my tears?

Absent of options
I stare
Into my
Powerlessness.

## What Do I Feel For You?

Like the Perseids meteor shower
I am awed and stare long
Drawn to you –
*How does she do that?*

While planning and paying
I am lifted up out of details
into sudden light –
*How does she do that?*

Warmed
by aggression yet
in the next moment deep affection –
*How does she do that?*

This morning I am surprised
by new courage to
face the short years ahead.
*How does she do that?*

## Prayer?

When I was younger
prayer was easy –
given words emptied the hour.

Soon
words were small, or
too long.

Later
anger and distance filled the space
between I and Thou.

Today
experience is the sacrament
that sanctifies my living.

Words
received in stillness
move me.

## Beauties

Some see beauty framed on walls
For others: NY sunrises or CA sunsets,
Curve of muscle, breast, or landscape.
*Hamlet*

Some see beauty in tireless generations
Growing toward clumsy harmony
Like a newborn colt.
*Take Five*

Some see beauty in truth finally told,
When they experience life
A little fuller.
*The Adventures of Tom Sawyer*

Then there are: David, The Great Barrier Reef
*Rhapsody in Blue* and the Temple at Luxor
Go ahead, you name two: _____, _____.

I know beauty by the catch in my breath
Heart stopping awe,
Flash of humbling nobility that comes:
Witnessing a triple play,
Cradling a life on its first morn!
A night alone with you,
Silver stars crowding a black Montana sky.
Can't count'em...

## Thank You Friends

Thank you for this island in time,
companions, seagull, pine tree, and wind.
I feel every corner of this stillness
on our little reach of sand,
at this confluence of currents in my life
[I have not been here before].

I am lifted up by story, by laughter, by
the tested courage in your steady gaze –
lifted off my eroding perch to be part of our mutual
river delta: your currents, your islands, many others too.

I again affirm the given gift of one river:
it doesn't matter which channel, what depth
is best or better -
I end up where I ought to be
[I have not been here before].

I throw away my worn oar
hold only your hands as
we float into the next now.

## Vulnerability

I was home sick last week
Four spring days in bed.
My wife asked, "What do you need?"
"A gun," I said.

One night, unable to sleep
I saw images on TV news
A powerful earthquake
Destroyed much of Katmandu.

A boy in a dirty shirt sat
In the Himalayan rain
Staring at a pile of bricks
Covering his family and simple domain.

His soaking pain is not punishment –
Nor my warm safety reward -
We share a breathing planet,
Brothers in our human state.

Whichever attentive god can hear -
Hindu, Muslim, or Jew -
Help us lean on our connection
And our courage renew.

## Spring Train To Portland

Sunset flicks through new alder leaves
phone lines stretch the miles away.
I slide by the shoreline
iron rhyme under my feet.

The sea, full in its spring tide
floats silent islands
in greens and browns
lifting and deepening my view.

The sun arches slowly
making shadows and gold on fallow fields.
I sense in some curious mounds*
layers of time, lost experience.

I beg a blessing of the trees:
*renew in me your poetry.*
In this time of asphalt and acid rain,
I share the insistence of you humble beings.

Now the sun strikes just the highest masts
and falls behind their guardian lines.
    Fatally wide-eyed
    finally awe struck
from this silver cocoon I rise!




*Mima Mounds: earthen shapes of unknown
 origin or purpose near Olympia, Washington.

## Holy Water

Gentle forest creek
messages stones and troubles
like warm oil slowly
worked into my skin

    …and drops
    thoughts
    from the flow of my
    now breath

        …while this hypnotic
        cascade surrounds me
        in safety.

            Control
            erodes away.

Later
free, fresh
I am slipped from
our world's womb.

## Who You Are In Me

If Life is a river and
God is the ocean
Then I am H 2
Your Oh!
In fluid tension
Splitting morning light
On this cherry blossom now

## Our Forest Cabin

Woodpecker leads the chorus as easter sun rises.
Ravens counterpoint in our cathedral of trees while
red squirrels solo loudly then debate.

This life song skates across her mirrored lake
bounces back to our weathered cabin
slicing my swollen heart.

I lean against the open door, cup in hand
breathing sharp freshness, spiced by spruce,
subtle fragrances with promise of spring.

This is holy ground, domed by timid blues
behind broken clouds beginning to blush.
Bitter coffee? mix of gratitude and grief?

>   *"A big piece of heaven!"*

Turned around by time, I image her smiling face
rising above the canvas tarp of our bed roll
then protected only by the first course of new logs.

>   *"...and this 360 view can't be beat!"*
>   She laughs waving one sweet arm around our 'bedroom'
>   - exposed to the world - at the edge of the forest.

>   Scent of that weeks' cut cedar logs
>   hung heavy in crisp morning dew.
>   The memory cuts deep, hurts good.

>   I was full of eager energy
>   empowered by her love of the lake.
>   First night, our new intimacy christened the site.

>   We worked through the lengthening days
>   as if we knew each other's hands and bodies -
>   together had built before.

>   Select, cut, trim, haul, notch, lift, set
>   sweat, kiss, mount, laugh/cuss, eat, then do it
>   again. And again. Together.

Walls slowly rose through summer days,
connection between us deepened
over decades.

"Good morning," slips out by habit.
I return to present on our threshold,
easing pain of hip and memory, feeling warmth inside.

*"First morning miracle!"* she insisted on such mornings
as if creation had just started –
a whole world new again.

I am no intellectual - never a theologian -
she was my needed spirit,
me, her part time pragmatist.

Now two years since her passing,
there are patches of slippery sadness,
silent empty spaces  in my world.

On this land I am filled, mysteriously renewed by
our cabin, smells and sounds of life around it -
another miracle.

# JOAN
*Celebrating Her Life*

Cracked crab, steamed just right
hot sourdough with butter enough
to feel big about.
*("It's a one butt kitchen!")*
 She ran her ship tight.

Mussels, clams, shrimp salad, an s'more
came out from her well stocked store.
Thanksgiving turkey with stuffing or stew,
all finished off with pressed coffee - philosophy too!
Her bountiful love was banquet for many a crew.

'was not the chef, but nurse, mother, soul friend, brought us 'round
'was her welcome smile, warm heart, sharp curious mind.
*("What ya reading? Here's a find!")*
All set off by sparkling blue eyes under
sail colored strands.

Later, a brood on her doorstep we did find:
three handsome lads; a lass, generous of beauty and mind.
Joan gathered them often out on the shore in
a leaky "boat house" over the water *("Just fine!")* -
now a compound for the clan, weathered memories to find.

'Tis from this shore we bid her farewell,
saw her slip slowly north out of sight.
She left us too soon – 'tis true – leaving us
many grand sprites: hair under sail, jaunty of dance,
eager to learn, a few with crystal blues.

> *"Home?"* she asked
> "Yes," he could say, at last.

She is home.

# Acknowledgements

### Photo Credits
I am inspired by the life and the art of **Jennifer Thompson**. Whether she is teaching art in Montana schools, juvenile detention facilities, or Nepalese villages high in the Himalayas, she radiates passion and contagious creativity. It is an honor to share this time and project together. Her eye and camera captured men aging consciously and courageously. jennifer@jenniferlthompson.com

### Cover Photos
**Kim Ebert** builds community with her hands: as a licensed massage therapist, a pasta maker, a music maker with her son, and a photographer. Her images, in both of my books, beautifully catch the spirit of the text and enhance it. bodysacred.com

### Book Design
**Susan Sezgin** is a neighbor, community activist, friend, wife, and mother. She also generously shares her creativity in web and book design. She is able to emphasize the nobility and humility of aging through her text layout, photo crafting and placement. She was the midwife for the vision that Jennifer and I brought to her. susan@susansezgin.com

### Poetry Editor
**JM Miller, M.F.A.**, is a gifted writer and teacher at the University of Washington Tacoma. An Eco Arts Award Grand Prize winner, JM sharpened my expression and widened my perception. janiem@uw.edu

### Photo Editor
**Jeff VanTine** teaches photography at Carroll College in Helena, Montana. In addition to teaching, Jeff's photographs have been published by The Nature Conservancy, Sierra Club, Montana Outdoors, and Northern Rockies Publishing. jeffvantine.com

### About the Author
Bill Kelly, M.Ed. lives in Tacoma, Washington where he and his wife Judy have had a private practice of self development workshops for men, women, and couples for over 33 years. As a youngster, Bill enjoyed being outdoors, especially in the mountains, and continues to find inspiration and renewal in wilderness areas as an 'old guy'. billkelly815@gmail.com

At billkelly815@gmail.com, you can order additional copies of this collection, Poems For Old Guys, Kindness is in Me (2012), and request information about poetry readings, classes, and retreats with the author.